CHECKS & BALANCES

Oren Safdie

I0139497

BROADWAY PLAY PUBLISHING INC
New York
www.broadwayplaypublishing.com
info@broadwayplaypublishing.com

CHECKS & BALANCES
© Copyright 2017 Oren Safdie

Cover art by Kinya Elenbarger

First edition: October 2017
I S B N: 978-0-88145-742-1

Book design: Marie Donovan
Page make-up: Adobe InDesign
Typeface: Palatino

CHECKS & BALANCES was first produced by
Arkansas Public Theatre—formerly Rogers Little
Theatre— (Ed McClure, Artistic Director) in Rogers,
Arkansas, opening in November 2012. The cast and
creative contributors were:

ELEANOR KAUFMAN..Joan Porter
JONATHAN SEGAL..Nick Abeel
VICTORIA WINSTON..................................Gameela Wright
GREGORY ZASLAVSKY .... Kris Pruett
KATHERINE LEITNER.............................. Kristen Begneaud

Directors .... Oren Safdie & Fritz Michel
Production manager .... Ed McClure
Business manager .... Kevin Lancaster
Lighting design .... Mike Manning
Costume design ....Brenda Nemec
Prop design .... Kathy McClure
Hair & make-up .... Randall Lothes
Set construction .... Jim Olmstead
Video projections from original paintings

....Kinya Elenbarger
Assistant stage manager .... Travis Mitchell
Stage manager...Autumn Trout

ACKNOWLEDGMENTS

Thank you to Ed McClure, the staff at Arkansas Public Theatre, and the city of Rogers, Arkansas, for making Checks & Balances' debut a memorable happening and the the-atre's first professional production. Much appreciation also goes to the Ellen Burstyn, Martin Landau and Mark Rydell at the Actors Studio West, Daniel Henning and Shelagh McFadden at The Blank Theatre, and Carol Ostrow and Jim Simpson at the Flea Theatre, for helping develop the play. Additional thanks go to the Canada Council for the Arts and the Québec Government Office in New York.

for Zilla Lippmann

CHARACTERS & SETTING

ELEANOR KAUFMAN, *into her 80s, a shock of white hair, she is a tough-minded, independent wealthy woman with a positive sense of humor. Her memory has begun to fail her but she doesn't let it frustrate her. In fact, sometimes it may seem that she has more control of her mind than she lets on. Despite diminished eye sight, poor hearing, and legs that just don't work like they used to, she remains full of poise and pride, and can even be a bit of a flirt in the company of a handsome young man.*

JONATHAN SEGAL, *a young, well-educated, music student in his 20s from Canada. He's somewhat of an idealist and tries desperately to be empathetic to other people's sufferings, which can come off as somewhat condescending. His overt sincerity can seem overbearing at times, if not too good to be true.*

VICTORIA WINSTON, *a Jamaican live-in maid in her 50s, she is almost what one might consider old school. She is polite, professional, and runs a tight ship. While at work, she wears a traditional maid's outfit (a light blue smock) and white nurse shoes. But as subservient as her job is, she has a strong backbone and knows where to draw the line.*

GREGORY ZASLAVSKY, *a Russian accountant in his early 50s. Not your typical C P A, he has a tumultuous past bottled up in his conservative suit. He wears square glasses and still speaks with a Russian accent even though he tries*

*to be more American than most Americans. His demeanor is
more Putin than Yeltsin.*

KATHERINE (KAUFMAN) LEITNER, ELEANOR's *daughter
is in her 50s, quite elegant, and has lived in Germany for
the past 20 years. But her mother's indifference has taken a
toll on her, and whenever in her presence, it brings out her
worst.*

Setting: New York

Time: Present

Scene 1

(JONATHAN *sits in the den, waiting. It seems as if he's staring out at the audience. After some moments,* VICTORIA *enters.*)

VICTORIA: Can I get you something to drink?

JONATHAN: No, that's fine, thanks. I wouldn't want to put you out.

VICTORIA: That's what I'm here for. A glass of water?

JONATHAN: Are you getting some for yourself?

VICTORIA: No.

JONATHAN: Some water would be great.

VICTORIA: With ice?

JONATHAN: If it's already made.

VICTORIA: We have other things too.

JONATHAN: Like what?

VICTORIA: Coke, 7-Up, ginger ale…juice.

JONATHAN: Fresh?

VICTORIA: Frozen.

JONATHAN: You know what, I'll stick with the water. And if you have something with bubbles, that's even better.

VICTORIA: Right away.

JONATHAN: No rush.

VICTORIA: Mrs Kaufman will be with you very soon.

JONATHAN: Tell her to take her time too. I'm a very patient person.

(VICTORIA *exits.* JONATHAN *waits, staring out, blankly. After some moments, he hears* ELEANOR *approaching from the hall, evident in the sound of a slight shuffle and dragging of her feet.*)

JONATHAN: (*Jumping up from his chair*) Hello, Mrs Kaufman.

ELEANOR: Hello?

JONATHAN: Hello, Hello.

ELEANOR: Who's that?

JONATHAN: It's me, Jonathan.

ELEANOR: T V repairman?

JONATHAN: No. Jon-a-than.

ELEANOR: Do I know you?

JONATHAN: We spoke briefly over the phone. I'm a friend of Paul Stein's.

ELEANOR: Is Paul here?

JONATHAN: No. I'm a friend of Paul's. He told me to say hello.

ELEANOR: Oh. How is Paul?

JONATHAN: He's fine.

ELEANOR: I should give him a call.

JONATHAN: Would you like me to?

ELEANOR: What?

JONATHAN: Dial his number?

ELEANOR: Who?

JONATHAN: Paul. Would you like me to call him?

ELEANOR: Why? Is something wrong?

JONATHAN: Not that I know of.

ELEANOR: We'll call him later. I like to check in with him from time to time, see how the Conservatory is doing. I write them a big check every year.

JONATHAN: Yes, I know.

ELEANOR: You do?

JONATHAN: I understand you were responsible for the new performance hall.

ELEANOR: Yes I was…

JONATHAN: Thank you.

ELEANOR: You're welcome…For what?

JONATHAN: I'm a student there.

ELEANOR: You are?

JONATHAN: Yes.

ELEANOR: Isn't that nice. What's your name again?

JONATHAN: Jonathan.

ELEANOR: Ralph?

JONATHAN: No, Jonathan.

ELEANOR: And what are you doing here?

JONATHAN: I've come about the job.

ELEANOR: What job?

JONATHAN: To help you with your bills.

ELEANOR: How did you hear about it?

JONATHAN: I'm a friend of Paul's.

ELEANOR: How is Paul?

JONATHAN: He's very well.

ELEANOR: Good, good…I'll have to call him.

JONATHAN: Later.

ELEANOR: Or maybe Thursday morning.

JONATHAN: I'll make a note of that.

ELEANOR: What?

JONATHAN: To call Paul.

ELEANOR: You're confusing me…

JONATHAN: Jonathan.

ELEANOR: Who's Ralph?

JONATHAN: I don't know.

ELEANOR: Well, are you staying?

JONATHAN: If you'd like me to.

ELEANOR: I'll tell Victoria to make up your bed.

JONATHAN: Oh, no, I'm not staying the night. I have my own place.

ELEANOR: As you should. Can you stand up please?

(JONATHAN *stands.*)

ELEANOR: Turn around.

(JONATHAN *turns around.*)

ELEANOR: Why aren't you wearing a suit?

JONATHAN: I didn't realize it was necessary for the position.

ELEANOR: What position?

JONATHAN: To help you with your bills, go through your mail.

ELEANOR: Good idea. Maybe we can open the mail.

JONATHAN: *(Relieved)* Yes! That would be nice.

ELEANOR: And then we should call…

JONATHAN: Paul?

ELEANOR: The man with the accent.

(JONATHAN *is confused.* VICTORIA *enters with a pitcher of water. He jumps up to try and help her with the tray.*)

VICTORIA: You can remain seated; I'll bring it to you.

ELEANOR: Oh, hello, Victoria. Have you met...

VICTORIA: Jonathan.

ELEANOR: Who?

JONATHAN: Jonathan. A friend of Paul Stein's.

ELEANOR: How is Paul?

JONATHAN: *(Trying to spell it out clearly for her in point form)* He's well. We'll call him later. He told me to come this afternoon because you needed someone to come once a week and help you with your bills. He said this was a paid position, and that you might throw in a free lunch.

ELEANOR: Well that settles that. Victoria, get this man some lunch. Have you met Victoria?

VICTORIA: *(Softly)* When he came in.

ELEANOR: Speak up!

VICTORIA: WHEN HE CAME IN—YOU FORGOT TO PUT YOUR HEARING AID IN.

ELEANOR: Don't need it today. I was just telling...

(ELEANOR *turns to look at* JONATHAN *for his name.*)

JONATHAN: JONATHAN!

ELEANOR: Right... So...

JONATHAN: JONATHAN!

(ELEANOR *turns to* VICTORIA *for clarification.*)

VICTORIA: VICTORIA!

ELEANOR: Now, I'm confused.

JONATHAN: Why don't I open the mail?

ELEANOR: Why don't you open the mail and we can see what I owe the world…

JONATHAN: I'll open the mail.

ELEANOR: Yes, that's a good idea. Open the mail. Would you like something to drink?

JONATHAN: Victoria already got me some water.

ELEANOR: Is that all?

VICTORIA: That was what he wanted.

ELEANOR: That's no way to treat our guest, Victoria. Why don't you make some lemonade?

VICTORIA: Right away.

ELEANOR: Do we have lemons?

VICTORIA: I believe so. Would you like some too?

ELEANOR: What time is it?

VICTORIA: Three O' clock.

ELEANOR: I think I'm ready for my coffee.

VICTORIA: It's a little earlier than usual.

ELEANOR: Why not. *(To* JONATHAN*)* I'm flexible.

*(*VICTORIA *exits.)*

JONATHAN: She's very nice.

ELEANOR: Who?

JONATHAN: Victoria.

ELEANOR: Oh, yes, she's from Jamaica. I don't know what I'd do without her. Been with me for…what year are we in now?

JONATHAN: 2012.

ELEANOR: Is it really?

JONATHAN: Yes.

ELEANOR: That makes me… *(Calculating in her head.)* …
pretty old.

JONATHAN: You look much younger.

ELEANOR: *(Challenging him)* Than what?

JONATHAN: Your age.

ELEANOR: How old am I?

JONATHAN: I don't know.

ELEANOR: Well, you're sweet anyway.

JONATHAN: Thank you.

ELEANOR: You're welcome… *(She grabs a tissue and
blows her nose.)* Now, tell me again, what's your name?

JONATHAN: Jonathan.

ELEANOR: Let me write that down. *(She fumbles around
on a side table and finds a pen and pad.)* Shoot.

JONATHAN: Jonathan.

ELEANOR: *(Doesn't need to write)* That's easy enough.
And what do you do?

JONATHAN: I'm a student at the Conservatory.

ELEANOR: Really. What instrument do you play?

JONATHAN: The euphonium.

ELEANOR: Don't know that one.

JONATHAN: E-flat baritone?

ELEANOR: Nope… And what have you come for?

JONATHAN: To help you with your mail.

ELEANOR: Do I need help?

JONATHAN: You said you did.

ELEANOR: When?

JONATHAN: Over the phone last week.

ELEANOR: Well, I suppose I do then.

JONATHAN: Would you like me to open the first letter?

ELEANOR: Of course, of course—wait, how much should we pay you?

JONATHAN: That's up to you.

ELEANOR: How's three dollars an hour?

JONATHAN: A bit low.

ELEANOR: Is it?

JONATHAN: Yes.

ELEANOR: Well, what are they getting these days?

JONATHAN: Paul Stein mentioned fifteen dollars.

ELEANOR: FIFTEEN DOLLARS!

JONATHAN: Paul Stein mentioned, yes.

ELEANOR: If Paul said fifteen dollars, I'm sure he had his reasons.

JONATHAN: Would you like to call him?

ELEANOR: For what?

JONATHAN: To corroborate.

ELEANOR: No, no, we'll leave it at…?

JONATHAN: Fifteen.

ELEANOR: FIFTEEN DOLLARS!!!

JONATHAN: Yes.

ELEANOR: You better be worth it.

JONATHAN: More than worth it.

ELEANOR: That's what I like to hear.

JONATHAN: Should I open the first letter?

ELEANOR: Please…

(JONATHAN *starts opening the letter.* ELEANOR *puts her leg up on his knee.*)

ELEANOR: Mind if I put my leg up on your knee?

JONATHAN: Ah—

ELEANOR: It helps the circulation.

JONATHAN: Sure.

ELEANOR: Are you a leg man?

JONATHAN: Excuse me?

ELEANOR: *(Proudly; about herself)* Oh, sure, it's nice to be pretty...but a good set of legs and a hearty laugh will take a girl a long way.

JONATHAN: I'm sure.

ELEANOR: Maybe you can rub my ankle.

(JONATHAN does, somewhat reluctantly.)

JONATHAN: Does that feel better?

ELEANOR: Much... And he's still alive?

JONATHAN: Who?

ELEANOR: The person we were talking about.

JONATHAN: I don't know.

ELEANOR: You don't know what?

JONATHAN: You wanted to know if someone is still alive.

ELEANOR: Most of them are dead.

JONATHAN: *(Taking the letter out of the envelope)* I'm opening the first letter.

ELEANOR: When I was a young girl, there was this handsome boy who used to write me the most beautiful letters.

JONATHAN: A boyfriend?

ELEANOR: I think he became my husband.

(VICTORIA brings in the coffee.)

ELEANOR: Victoria, what was the name of that man?

VICTORIA: Your husband was Richard. The man you were engaged to was Herbert.

ELEANOR: No, not him.

VICTORIA: And the young boy who wrote you the poems was Eugene.

ELEANOR: Eugene! That's the one. His father was a city councilor.

VICTORIA: No, that was Herbert.

ELEANOR: Right.

VICTORIA: Here's your coffee.

ELEANOR: What time is it?

VICTORIA: Just after three o'clock.

ELEANOR: It's a bit early, isn't it?

VICTORIA: I can bring it to you later if you like?

ELEANOR: That would be better.

(VICTORIA *exits, taking the coffee with her.*)

JONATHAN: The first letter.

ELEANOR: Bills on top, checks on the bottom.

JONATHAN: This is a donation request from English Inc.

ELEANOR: They must think I'm rich.

JONATHAN: These solicitations get mailed to everyone.

ELEANOR: Because I am, you know.

JONATHAN: …Yes, I know.

ELEANOR: Who told you?

JONATHAN: I assume since you give a lot of money to the Conservatory—*where I attend.*

ELEANOR: Do you know Paul Stein?

JONATHAN: Yes.

ELEANOR: How is he?

JONATHAN: *(Getting tired of this back and forth)* He's doing really really really well.

ELEANOR: But still no girlfriend.

JONATHAN: Not that I know of.

ELEANOR: *(Disturbed by the notion he might be gay)* Hmm… And what are you here for?

(JONATHAN slumps down in the chair, letting out a sigh.)

ELEANOR: *(Perking up; not wanting to lose him)* Right. The mail. Pay my Bills. My accountant—you know the one…

JONATHAN: No I don't.

ELEANOR: With the accent. He says it's good for me to make donations.

JONATHAN: Would you like to donate to these people?

ELEANOR: Who?

JONATHAN: English Inc.

ELEANOR: British pens?

JONATHAN: No. English Incorporated. They advocate making English the official language of the United States.

ELEANOR: Isn't it?

JONATHAN: I guess not.

ELEANOR: Well, what other languages are there?

JONATHAN: French, German, Chinese…a lot of Spanish.

ELEANOR: Let's give them some money. English is a good language to preserve.

JONATHAN: How much do you want to give?

ELEANOR: English Language…

JONATHAN: To make English the official language of the United States.

ELEANOR: Give 'em twenty bucks.

JONATHAN: So I write out the check?

ELEANOR: Yes, you write out the check, copy it down in the book with the amount and the date, and I'll sign it.

(VICTORIA *enters again with the lemonade.*)

VICTORIA: Here's your lemonade.

JONATHAN: Thank you, I hope I didn't—

VICTORIA: You didn't.

ELEANOR: Hello, Victoria.

VICTORIA: Everything okay?

ELEANOR: Fine. This is Jonathan. He's a friend of Paul Stein's from the Conservatory. Came over to help me with the bills. He plays the euphonium. Should we hire him?

VICTORIA: That's up to you, Mrs Kaufman.

ELEANOR: I think he's a keeper.

VICTORIA: Very well.

ELEANOR: Oh, and Victoria?

VICTORIA: Yes, Mrs Kaufman.

ELEANOR: I think I'll have my coffee now.

VICTORIA: Coming right up, Mrs Kaufman. *(She exits.)*

ELEANOR: Now, tell me again how do you know Paul?

(Black out)

Scene 2

(VICTORIA *stands, holding a tray of food. She starts shifting her weight from one foot to the next—and is about to sit when* JONATHAN *returns from the bathroom, zipping up his fly.)*

VICTORIA: I have your lunch.

JONATHAN: Sorry, I didn't realize you were waiting.

VICTORIA: It's no problem.

JONATHAN: I'm afraid the toilet's a little backed up.

VICTORIA: Don't worry—I'll take care of it. Would you like me to set the tray down on the coffee table?

JONATHAN: It might be better to leave it on the desk. I don't have much time today—I'm having a recital tomorrow evening.

VICTORIA: Is that like a concert?

JONATHAN: Yes. But we also get judged by our professors. It's open to the public—if you'd like to attend.

VICTORIA: That would be nice, but Saturdays are my only day off.

JONATHAN: Maybe next time.

VICTORIA: *(Interested)* What are you going to play?

JONATHAN: Elgar's Symphony No. 2 in E-Flat Major.

(VICTORIA *gives a polite nod that might suggest she is familiar with it.)*

JONATHAN: Do you know classical music?

VICTORIA: Not very well. But I enjoy the concerts at Lincoln Center.

JONATHAN: *(Surprised)* You go to concerts at Lincoln Center?

VICTORIA: Mrs Kaufman has season tickets to the New York Philharmonic.

JONATHAN: That's great. Do you go with Eleanor?

VICTORIA: Oh no, Mrs Kaufman hasn't gone out from the apartment in two years.

JONATHAN: *(Not meaning to be accusatory but coming out that way)* So she gives the tickets to you?

(VICTORIA is taken aback for a second.)

VICTORIA: Actually, it just so happens there's a concert next Saturday night. *(Going into the drawer, pulling them out and handing them to him)* Perhaps you'd like to take them.

JONATHAN: These are amazing seats.

VICTORIA: Fifth row, right in the middle.

JONATHAN: Shouldn't I ask Eleanor?

VICTORIA: She probably won't be up today. Had a rough night.

JONATHAN: What happened?

VICTORIA: Sometimes her saliva goes down the wrong passage and she can't stop coughing. Something to do with the valves in her throat. You just have to sit and hold her tight until she stops.

JONATHAN: You must be quite tired yourself.

VICTORIA: I'm used to it.

JONATHAN: Well, don't let me take up any more of your time.

VICTORIA: No problem.

JONATHAN: And if you get me the plunger, maybe I can—

VICTORIA: I'll take care of it later. *(She starts to leave.)* Let me know if you need anything else.

JONATHAN: Thank you. Right now I'm just familiarizing myself with everything.

VICTORIA: That's a good thing to do.

JONATHAN: So many documents to look through.

VICTORIA: Oh yes.

(Just as VICTORIA *is about to leave:)*

JONATHAN: Did you know Eleanor has two bank accounts that have been dormant for years?

VICTORIA: I didn't know that.

JONATHAN: I hope you don't mind, I went through all the statements and tried to put some order to things.

VICTORIA: I've been meaning to do that.

JONATHAN: Not that there's a lot of money in them but, still, the lost interest adds up.

VICTORIA: Every penny counts.

JONATHAN: I believe that too.

VICTORIA: I just realized, I forgot the gravy for your mashed potatoes.

JONATHAN: Please don't go to any trouble—

VICTORIA: It's already made, keeping warm on the stove.

JONATHAN: My mother would thank you—she always worries that I don't eat enough.

VICTORIA: Where does she live?

JONATHAN: Kingston, Ontario.

VICTORIA: Isn't that funny, I'm from Kingston, Jamaica.

JONATHAN: That's the *Common*-wealth for you.

*(*VICTORIA *doesn't get the joke.)*

JONATHAN: She's a Sociology professor at Queens University.

VICTORIA: I think I've heard of that.

JONATHAN: It's quite prestigious. My father teaches there too. English.

VICTORIA: You must be a very smart boy, coming from such good stock.

JONATHAN: Intelligence is overrated. All the miserable people I know are either educated or rich.

VICTORIA: That must be rough.

JONATHAN: I'm sorry, that sounded so elitist. I think I've just proven my point.

VICTORIA: Yes you have. I'll get you your gravy.

JONATHAN: Oh, and Victoria?

VICTORIA: Yes?

JONATHAN: Can I just ask you one more question?

VICTORIA: Of course.

JONATHAN: About the books.

VICTORIA: Yes.

JONATHAN: I'm just trying to understand how it all works.

VICTORIA: Are you having problems?

JONATHAN: Oh no, no problems at all. It's just...well ... there's all these checks...

VICTORIA: In my name.

JONATHAN: *(Relieved)* Yes.

VICTORIA: Whenever Eleanor needs something, she writes me a check. I cash it at the bank and buy whatever's needed.

JONATHAN: That's what I thought. Thanks.

VICTORIA: It's all listed by date.

JONATHAN: I see that. Perfect.

VICTORIA: Anything else?

JONATHAN: Um, no, I think that's— ...Actually, yes. Who's Moses?

VICTORIA: Moses is my husband.

JONATHAN: I see.

VICTORIA: Is there a problem?

JONATHAN: No, no, of course not. I just saw there were a few checks written to Moses Winston, so I wasn't sure what that was about.

VICTORIA: He does the handy work in the apartment.

JONATHAN: Okay. And Eleanor pays him for it.

VICTORIA: He's not going to do it for free.

JONATHAN: Of course not, that's a given. Just trying to familiarize myself with how everything works.

VICTORIA: She pays him twenty-five dollars an hour.

JONATHAN: So, the $443.75 on September 21 was for...

VICTORIA: To redo the bookshelves.

JONATHAN: So, that would be almost eighteen hours?

VICTORIA: Plus parts.

JONATHAN: The parts are extra?

VICTORIA: No, they're included in the total amount.

JONATHAN: Oh, okay, sorry. That makes sense. Maybe next time you can break it down so the figures reflect that.

VICTORIA: What do you mean?

JONATHAN: Just mark what is salary and what are parts.

VICTORIA: No problem...I'll get you your gravy now.

JONATHAN: If I can just have another teeny tiny second of your precious time...

VICTORIA: *(A little more aggravated)* What?

JONATHAN: Going back to Christmas...there's about three or four large checks of $3000 to numerous people.

VICTORIA: That must be to her grandchildren. Every year she sends them a gift.

JONATHAN: I see... But only $1000 to Katherine Leitner?

VICTORIA: That's her daughter. She lives in Germany.

JONATHAN: So she likes her grandchildren better than she likes her daughter?

VICTORIA: Isn't that usually the case?

JONATHAN: *(With a chuckle)* I suppose so...And eight thousand dollars to you.

VICTORIA: My Christmas bonus.

JONATHAN: And five thousand dollars to Moses.

VICTORIA: My husband's Christmas bonus.

JONATHAN: Right. Okay, I think I got it all now.

VICTORIA: *(In a frustrated way that makes Jonathan think twice about what she might do.)* Do you still want the gravy?

JONATHAN: Actually, maybe— ...Is Eleanor close with her grandchildren?

VICTORIA: Nicholas and Sabine live in Germany. They call every few months. She has another granddaughter from her son, Adam. He died last year.

JONATHAN: That's so sad. What from?

VICTORIA: Heart attack. His daughter drops by every so often, unannounced.

JONATHAN: Susan?

VICTORIA: Yes.

JONATHAN: I see a few small checks written out to her marked: phone bills, utilities, etc..

VICTORIA: She's trying to be an actress.

JONATHAN: And she lives in the city?

VICTORIA: Correct.

JONATHAN: I see... Do you have any children?

VICTORIA: One daughter.

JONATHAN: Latisha?

VICTORIA: How did you know?

JONATHAN: Oh, I just saw that there was a check for $9000 to The Neighborhood School and it said, "For Latisha's School" in parenthesis.

VICTORIA: *(Becoming more defensive)* Mrs Kaufman has been paying for my daughter's private education for many years. The family is well aware of it if you'd like to check with them.

JONATHAN: No, no, I wasn't implying they weren't— I'm simply trying to familiarize myself with everything... Understand how it all works. Take me for instance: I do X hours of work for Eleanor, I write up a check for my services to myself, and have Eleanor sign it?

VICTORIA: That's right.

JONATHAN: Is there anyone else I should be checking with— Or rather, is there anyone who is going to check on me to make sure everything is okay?

VICTORIA: Why shouldn't it be?

JONATHAN: In case I make a mistake.

VICTORIA: I don't follow.

JONATHAN: I mean, I'm an honest person—or at least I try to be—but is there anybody else who will make sure I'm not taking advantage of the situation?

VICTORIA: That's why we write everything in the book.

JONATHAN: Right. And then after the book is completed?

VICTORIA: You start another book.

JONATHAN: So there are other books?

VICTORIA: All of them are in the bottom right drawer. Going back three years.

JONATHAN: Okay. Great. That's all I was wondering. So, those books were looked at by...

VICTORIA: Mrs Kaufman's son.

JONATHAN: But now that he's no longer with us...

VICTORIA: I check them over at the end of the year and add them up.

JONATHAN: I understand—and not that there's anything wrong with that—but it's probably a good idea to have a system of checks and balances.

VICTORIA: What do you mean?

JONATHAN: It might be more appropriate for someone else to come in and take a look at the books other than you so that there aren't any misunderstandings.

VICTORIA: It's my understanding that that's why you're here.

JONATHAN: Yes, I suppose it is. I'm just wondering, aside from Eleanor's son—who is dead—is there anyone else who has been overseeing everything?

VICTORIA: You mean her accountant?

JONATHAN: Yes! Thank you. That's what I was looking for.

VICTORIA: Then why didn't you say so?

JONATHAN: Sometimes I have a hard time expressing what I'm trying to say. It's probably why I'm a musician and not a composer... So, this accountant comes in...

VICTORIA: Once a year, sometimes twice.

JONATHAN: And looks at the books.

VICTORIA: I assume so.

JONATHAN: And his/her name is...

VICTORIA: Gregory.

JONATHAN: Does he have an accent by any chance?

VICTORIA: (Concerned) You spoke with him?

JONATHAN: No.

VICTORIA: I think he's from Europe or somewhere like that.

JONATHAN: Do you know when he'll be coming next?

VICTORIA: Usually in March.

JONATHAN: So, the last time he was here was...

VICTORIA: Last March.

JONATHAN: About eleven months ago.

VICTORIA: Yes, that's about right.

JONATHAN: (Getting a little aggressive) But since that time—since her son died—there hasn't been anyone else here?!

VICTORIA: Why are you speaking to me in that tone?

JONATHAN: I'm sorry, you're right. Excuse my... inquisitively-natured enthusiasm. I'm just surprised that you've been put in this situation. It must be very stressful for you to juggle all these roles.

VICTORIA: (Now feeling like he's on her side) Yes it is.

JONATHAN: I mean, I see how much effort it takes to care for Eleanor, and if that's not enough, you've basically become the accountant, bank manager and personal assistant too.

VICTORIA: I'm glad you're able to appreciate the situation.

JONATHAN: So I'm going to try and alleviate some of that pressure from you.

VICTORIA: Thank you.

JONATHAN: For instance, I'll set up a charge account at the supermarket so all you'll have to do is sign, and I'll pay the bill at the end of the month.

VICTORIA: *(Concerned again)* Which grocery store?

JONATHAN: The Food Emporium, down the street.

VICTORIA: And what if I need to buy something they don't have?

JONATHAN: I haven't thought that through yet, but let me get back to you on that.

VICTORIA: Thank you.

JONATHAN: You're welcome.

VICTORIA: Your food must be cold by now. Would you like me to heat it up?

JONATHAN: Yes, please. And maybe I'll go for some of that gravy after all.

VICTORIA: With pleasure. Anything else?

JONATHAN: No, that's it.

VICTORIA: You're sure?

JONATHAN: Uh huh.

VICTORIA: Mr Segal?

JONATHAN: Please call me, Jonathan.

VICTORIA: I'm glad you're looking after Mrs Kaufman's books. She seems to like you.

JONATHAN: I like her too.

VICTORIA: It's important for her to be surrounded by people who care for her. That's what we all should hope for in our old age.

JONATHAN: Yes…it is.

(Black out)

Scene 3

(An expensive Japanese seafood restaurant. GREGORY *chews his food while looking over the books.* JONATHAN *sits in silence opposite him, taking an occasional bite of food himself, but always looking intently at* GREGORY *for any sort of reaction.)*

GREGORY: *(Finally, after swallowing; about the books.)* Did she see you take them?

JONATHAN: Definitely not. And I replaced them with blanks in case she opens the drawer.

GREGORY: Good thinking. *(Looking closer at the books)* Is this a one or a two?

JONATHAN: That's a three.

GREGORY: No kidding.

*(*GREGORY *reads on, while eating more. Suddenly, he looks up from the books; noticing* JONATHAN *isn't eating his food.)*

GREGORY: Is your food okay?

JONATHAN: Fine.

GREGORY: Because you didn't have to order the cheapest thing on the menu. It's on me.

JONATHAN: I like Chicken Teriyaki.

GREGORY: Here, try some of my uni; it's a real delicacy.

JONATHAN: No thanks.

GREGORY: I'm addicted to this stuff—reminds me of walking along a deserted, sandy beach at low tide.

JONATHAN: You like the sea?

GREGORY: All Russians like the sea. It's the only thing we didn't have to line up for. *(Back to the book)* ...See what she's done here? Her husband must've come in to do some work for a few hours on the 7th—see she's marked it to the nearest quarter of an hour—but then two days later, and three days after that, she's marked the exact same time allotment. Now, what are the chances of that happening?

JONATHAN: That figure includes parts.

GREGORY: Even more so. Most likely different repairs would require different parts. *(About to read on)* I have an idea, why don't we share an order of lobster. They're incredibly tender here—the chef sticks a chopstick up its ass while it's still alive to drain it of all its impurities. Makes the meat unbelievably tender.

JONATHAN: Really, I'm fine.

GREGORY: Seaweed salad? None of that slimy green stuff they sell in supermarkets. This is the real McCoy.

JONATHAN: No thanks.

GREGORY: *(Reading on.)* Cable-fine, D V Ds—a bit excessive, C Ds— *(Looking up)* By the way, what instrument do you play?

JONATHAN: The euphonium.

GREGORY: What's that?

JONATHAN: A baritone?

GREGORY: Never heard of it.

JONATHAN: Looks like a small tuba.

GREGORY: Then why don't you just play the tuba?

JONATHAN: What do you mean?

GREGORY: Well, if you have to describe an instrument as the lesser of another, there can't be much money in it, right? *(Excited)* What about something like the saxophone or the...trumpet!? Now, there's a sexy instrument. Miles Davis?

JONATHAN: In high school, my music teacher looked at my lips, asked me to blow, and assigned me to the euphonium.

GREGORY: Funny how life works. Now it's your career.

JONATHAN: I'm more comfortable in a supportive role.

(Not understanding this mentality, GREGORY shakes his head and goes back to reading the accounts.)

GREGORY: And these numbers here?

JONATHAN: My calculations are written in pencil. Victoria's are in pen.

GREGORY: Do the figures match up?

JONATHAN: To the penny.

(GREGORY closes up the book as if he's come to his conclusion.)

JONATHAN: ...So, what do you think?

GREGORY: You have to give it to her; she keeps a good book.

JONATHAN: That's what's so strange.

GREGORY: Not really. If you're a bank robber, do you walk into a bank dressed as a bank robber?

JONATHAN: Don't you want to check the figures over again?

GREGORY: You seem like an intelligent enough guy. Besides, numbers don't lie twice.

JONATHAN: Keep in mind, that total includes everything: salary, rent, food, clothing, and all other incidentals.

GREGORY: Eleanor eats Campbell's soup, she drinks Nescafe coffee, and she orders her dressing gowns from Sears. Even if she was partying every night with Beluga caviar and Dom Perignon, $156 000 in one year is uncomprehens… *(Unsure about the word)*

JONATHAN: Incomprehensible. I know, I know…

GREGORY: Feel like some dessert?

JONATHAN: No thanks.

GREGORY: They have incredible ice cream: red bean, green tea, ginger with real bits—all homemade.

JONATHAN: So what do you think we should do?

GREGORY: Is there really any question?

JONATHAN: I just think before we make any hasty decisions, it's important for us to weigh all the options and understand the implications.

GREGORY: I'm not sure I understand what you're getting at?

JONATHAN: Just that there are many things to contemplate before we take action. Some obvious, some not.

GREGORY: Such as?

JONATHAN: For instance, have we considered that, perhaps, Eleanor may have encouraged this escalation of payments?

GREGORY: Look at the checks. The signatures are barely legible. They start at the bottom of the page and curve up into the date. You really think Eleanor knows what she's signing?

JONATHAN: Maybe on a subconscious level.

GREGORY: So this is psychologic problem.

JONATHAN: No.

GREGORY: What we really should be doing is handing this over to the police.

JONATHAN: I can understand how you might feel that way.

GREGORY: And you feel differently?

JONATHAN: No. As I said, it's totally unacceptable. That's why I brought it to your attention.

GREGORY: Good.

JONATHAN: But there are larger issues we need to consider before we take action.

GREGORY: *(Repeating; with more challenge)* Such as?

JONATHAN: Eleanor's well-being.

GREGORY: She's living under the same roof with a back stabbing crook! If anything, we need to get Victoria out of that apartment a soon as possible and change all the locks.

JONATHAN: And then what?

GREGORY: I'll set up some interviews with other people tomorrow. I think I have the name of a good agency.

JONATHAN: And what about tonight?

GREGORY: Can you sleep there? I'm sure the family will compensate you.

JONATHAN: I'm not qualified to look after Eleanor any more than you are.

GREGORY: You're right… Maybe we'll leave it until the morning.

JONATHAN: More importantly, what about the morning after that?

GREGORY: What do you mean?

JONATHAN: Victoria has become much more than just Eleanor's maid. She's basically like family. And despite these monetary issues, I believe Victoria cares deeply for Eleanor. There's genuine affection between the two.

GREGORY: Dogs love their masters as long as they keep getting fed.

JONATHAN: That's unnecessary.

GREGORY: *(Sizing him up)* Why are you defending her?

JONATHAN: That's not my intention.

GREGORY: *(Grabbing the book and opening it and flipping through the pages)* I mean, the figures take off right after Adam drops dead and keeps climbing exponentially.

JONATHAN: I know, I know. I understand all that. There's no disputing she exploited the situation.

GREGORY: And that doesn't disturb you.

JONATHAN: It does. Deeply…I just don't see her actions as so black and white.

(GREGORY just stares at JONATHAN.)

GREGORY: I know English isn't my first language, but I'm having a hard time understanding what you're saying.

JONATHAN: What I'm trying to communicate to you is that…Victoria was left to make decisions for herself.

GREGORY: Go on.

JONATHAN: So maybe her excesses had something to do with the theatre she was operating in.

GREGORY: What theatre?

JONATHAN: The system.

GREGORY: Now you're really confusing me.

JONATHAN: An environment that was conducive to promoting her lax judgment.

GREGORY: *(Figuring it out)* Are you saying that I had something to do with this?

JONATHAN: Of course not.

GREGORY: Because that's what my sonar is picking up.

JONATHAN: Not at all. You obviously have many clients that put all sorts of demands on you. Paying day-to-day bills of an old lady is obviously not one of your responsibilities.

GREGORY: That's right.

JONATHAN: And if you can't trust people, how are you going to operate in life? No. There is no excuse for what she did.

GREGORY: Period!

JONATHAN: Period! …But I do think there was a slight lapse between the time of Eleanor's son's death and my arrival that allowed—maybe even encouraged—a person in Victoria's…circumstances to manipulate the operating theat— …the system—to her advantage.

GREGORY: You mean, to steal.

JONATHAN: Well, yes, technically it's stealing. But if you leave a piece of cheese in front of a mouse hole, are you going to be surprised that it's gone the next morning?

GREGORY: So we should judge her differently because she has the brains of a rodent?

JONATHAN: No. What I'm trying to say is that perhaps it's easy for us to judge her from where we stand.

GREGORY: I'm not following.

JONATHAN: The milieu we inhabit.

GREGORY: Once again?

JONATHAN: Our place of privilege.

GREGORY: What privilege are you talking about?

JONATHAN: Not necessarily privilege, but comparatively speaking, we obviously—

GREGORY: Do you know the first job they assigned to me when I arrived in this country?

JONATHAN: No.

GREGORY: I washed dishes for the first three years at some cheap Chinese restaurant in a neighborhood that looked like Mogadishu. I was mugged so many times that it got to the point where I'd just hold out the money in my hands so I wouldn't get my face slashed.

JONATHAN: My mistake, I had no idea.

GREGORY: You think I came here with ambitions of being an accountant?! ...Girls' eyes glazing over every time I tell them what I do for a living? I was a top physics student back in Moscow!

JONATHAN: Why didn't you continue?

GREGORY: I couldn't afford to go to college!

JONATHAN: They have scholarships.

GREGORY: Meaning, I couldn't afford to take time off work! My mother had asthma. She didn't speak English. I was responsible for bringing home the bacon. *Capiche*?

JONATHAN: I got the picture. Sorry.

GREGORY: So don't talk to me about privilege.

JONATHAN: It was stupid of me to assume—

GREGORY: Damn right it was! Who do you think you are?

JONATHAN: I completely deserve that, and I'm deeply sorry for presuming certain things about you. Please accept my apology... Sincerely.

GREGORY: *(Cooling off)* ...Apology accepted.

JONATHAN:.... *(Right back with his reasoning)* But just as I completely had no idea, and couldn't have any idea of what you went through to get to where you are today—what I'm saying is—we might not completely appreciate what it's like for a person in Victoria's position.

GREGORY: Because she has no working papers?

JONATHAN: That too.

GREGORY: My mother and I had to stand outside the American Embassy in twenty below zero temperatures for three months just to get a meeting. Don't get me started on the Illegals.

JONATHAN: But you got the meeting. You got to come to this country. You're a citizen now. You have no idea what it's like for people to treat you differently just because you're...

GREGORY: What?

JONATHAN: *(Not comfortable saying it)* ...Black.

(GREGORY looks at JONATHAN in disbelief.)

GREGORY: And you do?

JONATHAN: No. But I can empathize.

GREGORY: And that makes it all right for her to steal from an old, senile woman? Because of something that happened two-hundred years ago?

JONATHAN: Absolutely not.

GREGORY: Because fifty years ago her mother had to sit in the back of the bus?—I stand corrected, Victoria's not even from this country.

JONATHAN: Jamaicans were enslaved by the British.

GREGORY: Well, then, let's call up the British Consulate. Maybe they'll pay for this whole mess.

JONATHAN: People react differently to her because of the color of her skin.

GREGORY: People react differently to me because of my accent.

JONATHAN: Not in the same way.

GREGORY: And that justifies everything.

JONATHAN: No.

GREGORY: Then what are you saying?

JONATHAN: I'm telling you that all these factors— these different elements coming together at the same time—have created a situation that makes it a little more understandable. Not right! Just understandable. And in the interest of Eleanor, maybe we can work out something more constructive that will be affirmative to all parties involved. I mean, it's not like Eleanor has anyone to fall back on, and I certainly don't have the time or ability to assume responsibility for her.

GREGORY: Nobody's asking you to do that.

JONATHAN: Is it going to be you?

(GREGORY *considers this but puts his head down.*)

JONATHAN: I didn't think so!

GREGORY: *(Humbled)* So what are you proposing?

JONATHAN: People make mistakes.

GREGORY: Yeah, yeah, we've already gone through all that crap—get to the point.

JONATHAN: If Victoria's willing to accept responsibility for…being overly generous to herself-

GREGORY: Stealing.

JONATHAN: And she understands that she will have to make amends—

GREGORY: Pay it back.

JONATHAN: Then we will be willing to let her stay on.

GREGORY: And you think she's suddenly going to change her tune?

JONATHAN: No. But we can create a new system in which she is limited from access to Eleanor's funds. I've already set up an account at the supermarket.

GREGORY: So she'll buy groceries for the entire island of Jamaica and charge it to Eleanor.

JONATHAN: I'll monitor the situation. There will be no need for Victoria to ever write another check.

GREGORY: What about Eleanor's jewelry?

JONATHAN: I'll take stock of everything.

GREGORY: Books, records, artwork—some of it's quite valuable.

JONATHAN: I don't think Victoria has an appreciation for that. But if it makes you feel more comfortable, I'll archive all the titles.

GREGORY: You have it all figured out, don't you?

JONATHAN: I'm just trying to do what is in everyone's best interest.

(GREGORY *pauses, picks up the book again, and flips through the pages.*)

GREGORY: You're not from here either, are you?

JONATHAN: Born in Timmins, Ontario. It's a small town about two-hundred—

GREGORY: You're kidding me.

JONATHAN: What?

GREGORY: That's the birthplace of Pete Mahovlich.

JONATHAN: *(Surprised.)* How do you know that?

GREGORY: 1972. Final game of the Canada-Soviet Series. Mahovlich skates over to the scorekeeper's bench, climbs up into the stands, and waves his stick over the heads of three K G B agents... It was like lightning hit the Kremlin! Forget Reagan or Gorbachev, the collapse of the Soviet economy... Millions of Russians, watching their T V sets that night, in pure black and white, saw this young punk from Canada refuse to back down until they released his coach... Overnight, half of Russia wanted to move to Canada... It was my mother's first choice!

JONATHAN: Why didn't you go?

GREGORY: Unfortunately, you either had to speak French or have a hundred thousand dollars in your bank account... Ironically, the Americans couldn't care less what we had. Maybe they thought we'd be more appreciative.

JONATHAN: *And...in that spirit...can we give Victoria another chance?*

(GREGORY flips through the book again, but stops on a page. He zooms in on one specific entry.)

GREGORY: December 2nd. There's a check here for one hundred and twenty-six dollars, and twenty-eight cents.

JONATHAN: Christmas presents?

GREGORY: ...Toilet paper.

(GREGORY stares down JONATHAN who has nothing to say, and eventually looks down in defeat. GREGORY picks up the menu and opens it...)

GREGORY: I think I'll get the lobster for desert.

(Black out)

Scene 4

(JONATHAN *is pacing back and forth, looking to the
door in anticipation. He hears* ELEANOR *shriek from the
bedroom every so often—thinks about going to see what's
happening—but decides against it.)*

(Soon, ELEANOR *shuffles in, quite calmly, in fact, although
there is still a sense that something is not right.)*

ELEANOR: *(Not seeing* JONATHAN *but sensing his
presence.)* Hello?

JONATHAN: Hello, Eleanor.

ELEANOR: Hello?

JONATHAN: It's me, Eleanor.

ELEANOR: Who's there?

JONATHAN: It's Jonathan. Can I help you to your chair?

ELEANOR: I'm okay. *(She gets to her chair and sits with
some effort.)* Well, that's better isn't it?

JONATHAN: Yes.

ELEANOR: Is there anybody else in the room?

JONATHAN: Just me.

ELEANOR: You're sure.

JONATHAN: Positive.

ELEANOR: *(Bending over; almost whispering)* There's a
strange woman in my bedroom.

JONATHAN: That's Angelica.

ELEANOR: You know her?

JONATHAN: Yes.

ELEANOR: What does she want?

JONATHAN: She's helping you today.

ELEANOR: What happened to Victoria?

JONATHAN: She's taking the day off.

ELEANOR: Well, she's very nosy. She stood right in the doorway and watched me as I went to the bathroom.

JONATHAN: Does Victoria do that?

ELEANOR: What?

JONATHAN: Does Victoria stand in the doorway while you…

ELEANOR: Sometimes. But this one's very rough.

JONATHAN: I'll have a talk with her.

ELEANOR: What are you going to say?

JONATHAN: Not to be so rough.

ELEANOR: Better to just get rid of her… *(More chipper)* Now, what's the weather like today?

JONATHAN: It's a beautiful spring day. The sun is shining, the snow's melted, the birds are chirping. One of those days where it's hard to be angry at the world.

ELEANOR: Isn't that nice.

JONATHAN: Would you like to go out?

ELEANOR: Nah. My knees are a bit weak.

JONATHAN: I can take you in the wheelchair.

ELEANOR: Wheelchair!? For heaven's sake. I'll take a rain check.

JONATHAN: Whenever you want.

ELEANOR: You know where the word "rain check" comes from?

JONATHAN: No.

ELEANOR: When I was a little girl, my Uncle Joe used to take me to baseball games at the Polo grounds, and if it rained, they'd write you a rain check so you could come back another day. They'd scribble "rain check" right on your ticket.

JONATHAN: You like baseball?

ELEANOR: What's there not to like? Fresh air, green grass, men in uniform. My father used to sponsor a Little League club in New Jersey. Although nobody understood why since his furniture store was in Queens. The team was called the Maverics without a "k" —saved money on the stitching. *(More to herself)* Isn't it amazing I remembered that?

JONATHAN: Yes it is. Maybe I can arrange for us to go to a ball game together?

ELEANOR: I'll take a rain check...

(ELEANOR and JONATHAN share a chuckle.)

ELEANOR: Have you seen Victoria today?

JONATHAN: *(Lying)* No, Victoria has her day off.

ELEANOR: She needs it. Always on her feet doing something or the other—I don't know how she manages.

JONATHAN: Yes.

ELEANOR: I'm always telling her she works too hard.

JONATHAN: In fact, she might be gone a couple days.

ELEANOR: Oh?

JONATHAN: Could be a week.

ELEANOR: What about her sister-in-law?

JONATHAN: Her sister-in-law?

ELEANOR: She usually comes in on her day off.

JONATHAN: Right. She's away too. They both had some family function to attend to.

ELEANOR: Hope everything's all right.

JONATHAN: I'm sure it is.

ELEANOR: Maybe we should call her.

JONATHAN: Ah…

ELEANOR: Just to make sure she's okay.

JONATHAN: We can do that later.

ELEANOR: Because that one in there…

JONATHAN: Angelica.

ELEANOR: Very rough. Where did you find her?

JONATHAN: We can change her if it doesn't work out.

ELEANOR: What happened to Victoria's sister-in-law?

JONATHAN: She had to tend to the matter as well.

ELEANOR: What matter?

JONATHAN: A family get-together.

ELEANOR: I hope it's nothing bad.

JONATHAN: It's a reunion of some sort.

ELEANOR: Because it's not like her to leave without saying anything.

JONATHAN: (Getting in deeper) Actually, I believe she did.

ELEANOR: Did what?

JONATHAN: Tell you…that she…had to go away…for a few days.

ELEANOR: Oh? I don't remember that.

JONATHAN: Maybe you forgot.

ELEANOR: It's possible.

JONATHAN: I do it all the time.

ELEANOR: Because that woman in there—

JONATHAN: It won't happen again.

ELEANOR: She tried to clean me!

JONATHAN: Doesn't Victoria do that?

ELEANOR: Suppose so...but not so rough!

JONATHAN: She comes highly recommended.

ELEANOR: By who?

JONATHAN: Who?

ELEANOR: Who recommended her?

JONATHAN: Victoria thinks very highly of her.

ELEANOR: Yanked me right from the toilet seat, spritzed me with water, and shoved me in the corner.

JONATHAN: I'll have a talk with her.

ELEANOR: Are we paying her?

JONATHAN: It probably takes a few days for her to get used to a new person.

ELEANOR: Which person?

JONATHAN: You.

ELEANOR: I'm not following you. Can you get Victoria on the phone?

JONATHAN: She's unreachable.

ELEANOR: Look at my arms.

JONATHAN: What's wrong with them?

ELEANOR: Don't you see the marks? Yanked me from the toilet with such a force...

JONATHAN: (Getting up) I'll go talk to her right now.

ELEANOR: No, call Victoria.

JONATHAN: She didn't leave a number.

ELEANOR: There's a folder somewhere. It has all her information. Go get it.

JONATHAN: I don't know where it is.

ELEANOR: Never mind. Adam probably knows where it is.

JONATHAN: Adam?

ELEANOR: My son. Please call him. The number's in my black book on the table.

JONATHAN: Ah...

ELEANOR: Under K.

JONATHAN: Eleanor.

ELEANOR: Well, what are you waiting for?

(JONATHAN *gets up and goes over to the desk.*)

ELEANOR: If he's not home, you can try him up at the lake.

JONATHAN: It's probably going to be hard to reach him.

ELEANOR: What day is it today?

JONATHAN: Friday.

ELEANOR: He'll be there. Leaves on Thursday comes back Saturday. Beats the traffic. Of course, when we used to go up, there wasn't any traffic to worry about. (*Turning to* JONATHAN) Did you find the number?

JONATHAN: Eleanor—

ELEANOR: Why aren't you calling?

JONATHAN: Adam passed away last year.

ELEANOR: Oh? ...Oh, yes he did, didn't he. Well, I'm sorry you won't get a chance to meet him.

JONATHAN: Me too.

ELEANOR: You would've liked him.

JONATHAN: I'm sure... Would you like to call Katherine?

ELEANOR: No, that's all right. It's usually too late to call Europe. Who should we call?

JONATHAN: Do you want to call Paul Stein?

ELEANOR: How do you know Paul?

JONATHAN: From the Conservatory.

ELEANOR: And your name is…

JONATHAN: Jonathan.

ELEANOR: Ralph?

JONATHAN: *(Giving in)* …Yes.

ELEANOR: Now you're confusing me. Did Victoria say when she's coming back?

JONATHAN: No.

ELEANOR: I hope everything's all right. She pushes herself too hard.

JONATHAN: I'm sure it's fine.

ELEANOR: How do you know?

JONATHAN: It seemed like a happy occasion.

ELEANOR: It's not like her… And this one's very rough.

JONATHAN: I'll look into getting somebody else.

ELEANOR: Why do we need somebody else?

JONATHAN: In case Victoria is gone for longer than expected.

ELEANOR: *(Calling out)* Victoria!

JONATHAN: She's not here, Eleanor.

ELEANOR: I don't believe you…Victoria!!

JONATHAN: Eleanor, Victoria isn't coming back.

ELEANOR: Why not?

JONATHAN: She's gone back to Jamaica.

ELEANOR: With Latisha?

JONATHAN: Yes, with Latisha. And Moses too.

ELEANOR: What about school?

JONATHAN: They found a really good school in Jamaica.

ELEANOR: Why didn't she say good-bye?

JONATHAN: She did! Don't you remember?

ELEANOR: No, she didn't. You're lying.

JONATHAN: Okay, she didn't. But she told me to tell you—

ELEANOR: Victoria!

JONATHAN: She was stealing, Eleanor!

ELEANOR: Vic—! *(A matter of fact)* She was?

JONATHAN: Yes! She stole a lot of money from you.

ELEANOR: Are you sure?

JONATHAN: Yes.

ELEANOR: Well, then, she'll just have to give it back.

JONATHAN: It's not that simple.

ELEANOR: Maybe we weren't paying her enough.

JONATHAN: You were paying her plenty.

ELEANOR: I'll have to have a talk with her.

JONATHAN: She's gone.

ELEANOR: I'm rich, you know.

JONATHAN: I know.

ELEANOR: It's my money!

JONATHAN: Yes it is.

ELEANOR: Bring her back.

JONATHAN: I can't.

ELEANOR: That one in there nearly killed me!

JONATHAN: We'll find somebody else.

ELEANOR: Glaring at me while I went to the bathroom. She tried to wipe me!

JONATHAN: She's fired! Okay?

ELEANOR: Why did you send her away?

JONATHAN: It was over a hundred thousand-

ELEANOR: *(Overlapping)* I'm not listening to you whoever you are. *(She blocks her ears; in protest.)* Victoria!

JONATHAN: There's nothing I can do.

ELEANOR: Victoria!...

(Suddenly, ELEANOR's protest turns into a coughing fit; JONATHAN tries to hold her.)

ELEANOR: Get your hands off me!

(Now ELEANOR's coughing has made it impossible for her to get a word out. JONATHAN just holds her tightly. She finally stops coughing for a moment, but gasps for air.)

ELEANOR: I want Victoria.

JONATHAN: I know.

ELEANOR: Get Victoria.

JONATHAN: I'll see what I can do.

(Black out)

Scene 5

(A park bench. Although it's still April, the weather has turned colder. A few snowflakes fall. VICTORIA sits bundled up, looking cold and impatient. After several moments, JONATHAN shows up carrying his euphonium case.)

JONATHAN: I'm sorry to keep you waiting—my instructor let us out late.

VICTORIA: *(Impatient and obviously hurt)* What do you want?

JONATHAN: How are you feeling?

VICTORIA: What do you care? Now, what do you want?

JONATHAN: I'm sorry things have unfolded the way—

VICTORIA: What way?

JONATHAN: The way that they have.

VICTORIA: I was thrown out of my room like I was a common criminal.

JONATHAN: That wasn't my intention.

VICTORIA: Nothing happens on its own. Now, what do you want? I don't have much time.

JONATHAN: I would like to give you an opportunity—

VICTORIA: *(Snapping)* An opportunity for what?

JONATHAN: Please let me finish.

VICTORIA: Go ahead.

JONATHAN: Understand, I'm representing many people's interests here.

VICTORIA: And what's your interest?

JONATHAN: Eleanor is my interest.

VICTORIA: *(Repeating)* An opportunity for what?

JONATHAN: To admit…

VICTORIA: …something I didn't do? Where's the opportunity in that?

JONATHAN: Please let me finish what I have to say and then you can retort all you want.

VICTORIA: What does that mean?

JONATHAN: Yell at me.

VICTORIA: *(Furious but containing it)* …Speak.

JONATHAN: First thing I want to say—to convey directly to you—is that despite the way things may appear, I'm actually surpassingly partial to your point of view.

VICTORIA: Meaning?

JONATHAN: I'm on your side.

VICTORIA: My side?

JONATHAN: Stay with me, please.

(VICTORIA *contains herself.*)

JONATHAN: I feel for what you're experiencing right now. More importantly, I feel for what you've had to endure your entire life.

VICTORIA: What do you know about my life?

JONATHAN: I know absolutely nothing about your life. I don't even pretend to know. But I—

VICTORIA: —know nothing.

JONATHAN: Right. But I would hope that I am still capable of empathizing with—

VICTORIA: What?

JONATHAN: Sympathizing with—

VICTORIA: Being a maid?

JONATHAN: Empathizing, yes...

VICTORIA: *(Amazed)* Really?

JONATHAN: I would like to think so.

VICTORIA: So you know how it feels to be a stranger in the place you sleep six nights a week? Visitors coming and going, not remembering your name, like you're invisible, there to take their coat and serve them a drink? Maybe unclog their toilet? Or how, over time, this becomes normal, you accept it as part of the job and without even knowing it, you wake up one day

and realize you no longer recognize who you are? Can
you *empaphize* with that? Because that's what this job
demands. We exist to take care of your old, your sick
and service all your needs. Oh, no, we're not slaves
anymore. We get paid! But our lives, our families, our
dreams—the normal things in a person's life—are
sacrificed to make sure your lives are comfortable. The
maid across the hall at Mrs Vallero's—she's from the
Philippines—back home she has five children that are
being brought up by her sister. Hasn't seen them in six
years. The youngest doesn't even know she exists—
they thought it would be easier that way.
Upstairs at Mrs Lansing's, she has a new driver from
Guatemala—couldn't afford to take time off work and
fly home to bury his own father. Oh sure, they tell you
you're just like one of the family, but only if you leave
your own behind. God forbid a husband wants to
spend the night with his wife, or a child drops by after
school while the guests are still over. And the thing
is when your "Master" finally does kick the bucket,
there's no holiday, no promotion, no retirement. Now
you have to look for a new job. And the new boss don't
care how long you've been working, or how much
you got paid at your last job. Half the time it's the
children doing the hiring and the only thing they care
about is saving their parent's money for themselves.
And there's a whole city out there, swarming with
desperate people, willing to do anything for half the
price no matter how low you're willing to charge.
Some even have nursing certificates. So after all your
hours of cleaning toilets, sweeping floors, washing
bed stains, and wiping big fucking white asses, you're
no better off than when you first stepped off the boat.
Now, you tell me how you can possibly *empaphize* with
anything in my life?

JONATHAN: *(After a beat)* Wow... What can I say?

VICTORIA: Nothing!

JONATHAN: ...I'm ashamed.

VICTORIA: Damn right. You should be ashamed.

JONATHAN: Not only for myself, but also for this opulent, narrow-minded society we live in.

VICTORIA: I'm talking about you, right here.

JONATHAN: I accept that. Totally. Completely. One-hundred percent. But I also think it's important for me to express to you that I believe this is a much bigger problem than just you or me. And from everything you just said, I can honestly say that you have convinced me, unequivocally, that if I were in your shoes, I would have felt compelled—even justified—in doing what you did.

VICTORIA: What I did?

JONATHAN: I mean, what responsible mother would not have done the same thing for the well-being of her child?

VICTORIA: But I didn't do anything!

JONATHAN: Of course you didn't... That's my point. *It* did it to *you*. That's why it's important for you not to fall into their trap.

VICTORIA: Who's trap?

JONATHAN: The people in charge. The authorities. The system. The ones who are trying to keep people like you from getting ahead. You have to be smarter than them because they're just waiting for you to mess up.

VICTORIA: But you were the one who took the books to Gregory.

JONATHAN: Yes I did.

VICTORIA: You took them to him!

JONATHAN: I admit that. Without even thinking of
the implications, my initial reaction was to take these
books to the accountant and rat you out.

VICTORIA: Why?

JONATHAN: I know this might be hard for you to
comprehend, but as much as I sympathize with your
circumstance, I, unfortunately, am also a part of the
system. And I hate myself for that. So, yes, I would do
exactly as you did, but I would also be the first to turn
myself in. That's just the way I've been conditioned by
the greater forces that control our society.

VICTORIA: But I didn't do anything—

JONATHAN: *(Losing patience)* Victoria—

VICTORIA: It was all given to me—

JONATHAN: *(Showing a more aggressive side)* There was
over a hundred thousand dollars written out to your
name. You're lucky I was able to convince them not to
press charges.

VICTORIA: Go ask Eleanor. She signed every one of
those checks herself.

JONATHAN: *(Abandoning the last of his reasoning tone)* Oh,
come on, Victoria! It doesn't take a brain surgeon to see
that her mental capacities are not operating at optimal
levels.

VICTORIA: She understands more than you think.

JONATHAN: She doesn't remember my name half the
time!

VICTORIA: Well, she remembers mine! She knows how
many years I've been working for her. She understands
that of all the people in her life, I'm the only one she
can depend on. And if she wanted to compensate me
for that, what's wrong with that, huh? What's wrong
with making sure I have some money to retire with, or

that my daughter gets a college education? Or that my husband can afford to see a good doctor? Can you tell me what's so wrong with that?

JONATHAN: If you didn't feel you were being properly compensated, there were other channels you could've pursued.

VICTORIA: Like what? Asking her daughter? Last time she was here, she took me to the supermarket and showed me how I could save fifteen cents on a can of tuna if I bought the brand made by the store.

JONATHAN: I'm sure Gregory would have—

VICTORIA: The accountant? The one time I asked him for a raise, he told me that I should feel lucky to have such a cushy job. Eleanor asked him if maybe my husband and I could apply for working papers; he told her it wasn't worth the effort… When Eleanor goes, there's nothing left for me. She understands that.

JONATHAN: And so do I.

VICTORIA: No, what you understand, and have always understood—growing up in your privileged world— is that if anything goes wrong, there is a net to catch you. If you get sick, you know you're not going to die in the street. If you lose your job—or never get one— you won't end up at the shelter with your child… But there's no net to catch me. There's nothing there if I fall. There are only people who are depending on me to catch them. (She gathers herself as if she's about to leave. One last word) I've earned that money… Seventeen years… Oh, yes, I earned it big time!

(Just before VICTORIA leaves…)

JONATHAN: To what end?

VICTORIA: What?

JONATHAN: Where do you draw the line? How much would it take to make you feel like it's a fair deal?

VICTORIA: Eleanor wanted me to be comfortable, that's all.

JONATHAN: Yes, she did. There was a small piece of property on Long Island she was going to leave you.

VICTORIA: *(Shocked)* You're lying.

JONATHAN: For legal reasons, it was put in Latisha's name.

VICTORIA: The family would never let it happen.

JONATHAN: If you return the money, you can be back at work tomorrow.

VICTORIA: It's not possible.

JONATHAN: It doesn't have to be in one lump sum, we can arrange a payment schedule that will take a little out of your paycheck every week.

VICTORIA: I need that check to pay for Latisha's expenses.

JONATHAN: Say a hundred dollars a week.

VICTORIA: It's not possible.

JONATHAN: Fine. Then get it from the money you put away.

VICTORIA: There is no money put away!

JONATHAN: Look, Victoria, I'm willing to work with you, but you have to be straight with me...

(VICTORIA *feels out the situation.*)

JONATHAN: I want to help.

VICTORIA: *(Very emotional)* My husband, he...

JONATHAN: Spent it?

VICTORIA: Lost it.

JONATHAN: What do you mean? How do you lose something like that?

VICTORIA: He bought a computer. Signed up with one of those day-trading accounts, where you buy and sell things with the push of a button.

JONATHAN: *(Shocked)* You're kidding.

VICTORIA: He was so proud—he wrote people at home that he was the owner of this company, thinking of buying that company.

JONATHAN: All of it?

VICTORIA: You see, when we first arrived in this country from Jamaica, everyone back home expected we'd do great things...I remember the first night we walked down Fifth Avenue and looked in the windows of all the fancy shops. It was Christmas. We felt there was nothing that could hold us back... Relatives back home waited for news. They opened our letters and wanted to read about how wonderful we were doing, and how we were doing depended on how much green we put in the envelope... At the beginning, we sent all we could because we were sure that there was going to be more...But then it didn't come... We sent less... They stopped writing.... All my husband wanted was for people to start writing us again... Is that such a crime?

JONATHAN: *(Disgusted; feeling betrayed)* I was on your side. *(He picks up his euphonium case and exits.)*

(VICTORIA slumps back down on the bench and stares out as if she has no idea what to do next. It starts snowing harder.)

(Black out)

Scene 6

(ELEANOR *is sitting in her chair in the den, appearing to stare out at the audience. After some moments,* JONATHAN *enters with a beautiful arrangement of yellow buttercup flowers, placed in a vase. He sets them down on the table.*)

JONATHAN: There we go. Much better.

ELEANOR: Oh, those are gorgeous. What kind are they again?

JONATHAN: Buttercups. And they have a wonderful smell to them too.

ELEANOR: Do they?

JONATHAN: Should I bring them closer?

ELEANOR: No, they're perfect right where they are. Do they need a vase?

JONATHAN: *(Holding it up for her)* They're already in one. See?

ELEANOR: I was looking all over for that the other day. Where did you find it?

JONATHAN: Rosalia gave it to me.

ELEANOR: Is she in the kitchen?

JONATHAN: Yes, she's getting our lunch ready.

ELEANOR: Is she?

JONATHAN: Some kind of lamb with tomatoes and peppers. Looks very good.

ELEANOR: I can't eat spices.

JONATHAN: She knows that.

ELEANOR: *(Almost impressed)* Does she?

JONATHAN: Yes.

ELEANOR: Good.

JONATHAN: ...So everything's working out with her?

ELEANOR: I suppose.

JONATHAN: And she's gentle?

ELEANOR: What do you mean?

JONATHAN: In the bathroom.

ELEANOR: What do you mean?

JONATHAN: After you've done your business.

ELEANOR: *(Protecting her pride)* That's none of your business.

JONATHAN: Sorry.

(Pause)

ELEANOR: *(Looking at the flowers)* A gorgeous color!

JONATHAN: Aren't they? The second I saw them, I knew I had to buy them for you.

ELEANOR: You're spoiling me.

JONATHAN: You deserve it.

ELEANOR: Aren't you sweet.

JONATHAN: Actually, I'm really mean, nasty and horrible, but I have everyone fooled.

(ELEANOR *lets out a loud chuckle.*)

JONATHAN: Well, someone's in good spirits today.

ELEANOR: Am I?

JONATHAN: At least you seem to be.

ELEANOR: Be what?

JONATHAN: In good spirits.

ELEANOR: *(Declarative)* I am.

JONATHAN: Great. Any special reason?

ELEANOR: Not that I can remember.

JONATHAN: Well, sometimes it's like that.

ELEANOR: Like what?

JONATHAN: For no particular reason. They now say it has to do with hormones.

ELEANOR: *(Remembering)* I had the funniest dream last night…that I was skating in Central Park.

JONATHAN: Did you used to skate?

ELEANOR: Never.

JONATHAN: But you could skate in your dream?

ELEANOR: Oh, sure, like a dream… And when I woke up, I felt so light.

JONATHAN: *(Suggestive)* Like a great weight had been lifted from your shoulders?

ELEANOR: No, not like that.

JONATHAN: Like your mind was free of any burdens?

ELEANOR: No… When I was a young girl, there used to be this very handsome boy who used to come by the house and ask me to go out with him in his canoe that he built with his own hands. My mother always said no, of course, but I would sneak out and meet him by the neighbor's dock, and we would paddle out to the middle of the lake and just drift to wherever the lake wanted us to go… Like that.

JONATHAN: Was that Eugene?

ELEANOR: Herbert.

JONATHAN: The man you were engaged to.

ELEANOR: *(Impressed that he knows)* That's right.

JONATHAN: What happened to him?

ELEANOR: I'm not sure. *(Trying to be cheery but still somewhat painful)* I think he went off and married someone else.

JONATHAN: I find that hard to believe.

ELEANOR: So did I… *(Reminiscing; with a tinge of jealousy)* But she sure did have a hearty laugh.

(JONATHAN gets up and fixes the flowers so they fan out.)

JONATHAN: Gives them a little more room to breathe.

ELEANOR: *(About the flowers)* Pure heaven… *(Sizing him up)* But you've grown since the last time you were here.

JONATHAN: I…don't think so.

ELEANOR: Yes you have. What's your size?

JONATHAN: Forty-two.

ELEANOR: Is that the same size as your grandfather?

JONATHAN: Actually, he's a bit bigger.

ELEANOR: I don't think so. You should go into the bedroom and try on some of his old suits. There's a whole closet filled with them.

JONATHAN: *(Realizing she is mixed up)* Ah…

ELEANOR: They're just sitting there getting eaten by moths.

JONATHAN: Eleanor…

ELEANOR: Go on. You can take what you want.

JONATHAN: But—

ELEANOR: It won't hurt you to try them on.

(JONATHAN exits toward the bedroom and comes back after a few moments.)

ELEANOR: Did you find anything you like?

JONATHAN: They weren't there.

ELEANOR: *(Not sure what he's referring to)* What?

JONATHAN: Your *husband's* suits.

ELEANOR: Go ask Victoria. Maybe she moved them to another closet.

JONATHAN: I don't want to bother her. She's fixing lunch.

ELEANOR: All right. But remind me to ask her.

JONATHAN: I will.

ELEANOR: *(About the flowers)* And they smell wonderful too.

JONATHAN: Yes they do... *(Trying to get conversation back on track)* So, what did your *husband* do?

ELEANOR: Printing business.

JONATHAN: Is that how he made his fortune?

ELEANOR: Oh, no, the money's mine. From my Uncle Joe—he was a famous record producer. Had no children of his own.

JONATHAN: Didn't he found the Conservatory?

ELEANOR: How do you know about the Conservatory?

JONATHAN: I'm a student there.

ELEANOR: Isn't that a coincidence!

JONATHAN: Yes.

ELEANOR: What instrument do you play?

JONATHAN: The euphonium, sometimes known as an E-flat baritone.

ELEANOR: Oh, sure, it's a wonderful instrument. Never gets the attention of the tuba, not quite as flashy as the trombone, but it has a very smooth tone.

JONATHAN: *(Affirmation)* Exactly!

ELEANOR: Do you have a nice suit?

JONATHAN: What do you mean?

ELEANOR: When you perform in a concert?

JONATHAN: It's pretty old, but it does the trick.

ELEANOR: I have some wonderful suits in the closet.

JONATHAN: They weren't there.

ELEANOR: Oh, right... Well, let me write you a check so you can get yourself a new one.

JONATHAN: That's okay.

ELEANOR: Every serious musician should have a nice black suit.

JONATHAN: It's really not necessary.

ELEANOR: I won't take no for an answer. Now, go over to the desk and bring me my checkbook.

(JONATHAN *heads for the desk, but then turns back with an idea.*)

JONATHAN: I know, why don't I go take a look at your husband's suits?

ELEANOR: We gave them away years ago. Besides, you need something new.

JONATHAN: I really don't feel comfortable—

ELEANOR: *(Sternly)* Don't argue with me.

(JONATHAN *hesitates, but then goes over to the table and retrieves the checkbook.*)

ELEANOR: How's four hundred dollars?

JONATHAN: Much too much.

ELEANOR: Do you have a white shirt?

JONATHAN: Yes.

ELEANOR: What about black shoes?

JONATHAN: Dark brown.

ELEANOR: *(Like it's a sin)* Brown with black? That's horrible. Make it five hundred.

JONATHAN: I can't accept that.

ELEANOR: Sure you can.

JONATHAN: It's better if we keep things separate-

ELEANOR: Keep what separate?

JONATHAN: It's just that I'm working for you.

ELEANOR: Are you really?

JONATHAN: Yes.

ELEANOR: When's your birthday?

JONATHAN: Not until the fall.

ELEANOR: That's right around the corner. Now, write the check out to yourself and I'll sign it.

(JONATHAN *hesitates.*)

ELEANOR: Go on.

(JONATHAN *writes it out.*)

ELEANOR: *(As he's writing)* Don't forget to... *(To herself)* What is it you have to do?

JONATHAN: ...Mark it down in the ledger.

ELEANOR: That's right.

(JONATHAN *hands* ELEANOR *the check.*)

ELEANOR: Where's the signature line?

JONATHAN: *(Pointing)* Right there.

(ELEANOR *signs it.*)

ELEANOR: *(Handing it to him)* There you go.

JONATHAN: *(Accepting the check)* Thank you.

ELEANOR: Mark it in the ledger.

JONATHAN: I did.

ELEANOR: You're welcome.

(JONATHAN *takes the checkbook back to the table and places it on the desk. He looks at the check and rips it into pieces, throwing it into the garbage. He then returns to the chair next to* ELEANOR.)

ELEANOR: I don't know about you, but I'm feeling hungry.

JONATHAN: She's getting lunch ready.

ELEANOR: Who?

JONATHAN: *(Not sure who to mention; then, taking a chance.)* ...Rosalia?

ELEANOR: You know, I have a hard time remembering her name.

JONATHAN: Think of the flower.

ELEANOR: That's very clever. I'll do that. *(Regarding the buttercups)* Beautiful color.

JONATHAN: I knew you'd like them.

ELEANOR: Do you buy flowers for your wife?

JONATHAN: I'm not married.

ELEANOR: That's terrible of me, I keep forgetting... She was a very sweet girl.

JONATHAN: Ah... (Playing along this time. Yes.

ELEANOR: What was her name again?

JONATHAN: *(Mumbling so it's inaudible)* Ambingdena?

ELEANOR: That's right... But your sister's well?

JONATHAN: Yes.

ELEANOR: Any boyfriends?

JONATHAN: *(Guessing)* Not that I know of.

ELEANOR: Good for her. A young lady needs time to herself. *(Pause)* What's she doing in there? I'm getting hungry.

JONATHAN: I'll go see what's holding things up.

ELEANOR: Don't bother getting up. *(Yelling out)* Victoria! We're ready for lunch!

JONATHAN: I'm sure *Rosalita* will bring it out as soon as it's ready.

ELEANOR: I thought her name was Rosalia.

JONATHAN: Rosalia, right!

ELEANOR: Think of rose petals.

JONATHAN: Good idea.

ELEANOR: And you should really think about getting married again. You're not getting any younger.

JONATHAN: I know, I know.

ELEANOR: Do you have a nice suit?

JONATHAN: Yes.

ELEANOR: There's a whole closet of them in the bedroom. What size are you?

JONATHAN: Forty.

ELEANOR: Too small. Let me write you a check so you can buy yourself a new one.

JONATHAN: It's okay, I have three wonderful new suits.

ELEANOR: A black one?

JONATHAN: Black, white, navy blue.

ELEANOR: Every young man should have a gray suit. Do you have a nice dark gray suit?

JONATHAN: No.

ELEANOR: Bring over the checkbook.

JONATHAN: Eleanor...

ELEANOR: I can afford it. I'm rich, you know.

JONATHAN: I know. You write a big check to the Conservatory every year.

ELEANOR: How did you know?

JONATHAN: I'm a student there.

ELEANOR: Paul Stein let me buy him a suit.

JONATHAN: He did?

ELEANOR: Sure… Several times.

JONATHAN: …Okay, fine. *(He brings the checkbook over.)*

ELEANOR: How's six hundred dollars?

JONATHAN: Two hundred is more than enough.

ELEANOR: Two hundred? No serious musician would be caught dead in a two hundred dollar suit.

JONATHAN: How much was Paul's suit?

ELEANOR: Paul?

JONATHAN: Paul Stein.

ELEANOR: Now you're confusing me.

JONATHAN: You said you bought Paul Stein a suit.

ELEANOR: Yes I did.

JONATHAN: How much did you pay for his suit?

ELEANOR: That's between Paul and I.

JONATHAN: Sorry.

ELEANOR: Now, write out a check for seven hundred dollars and I'll sign it.

(JONATHAN writes out the check and hands it to ELEANOR to sign.)

ELEANOR: Can you—

(JONATHAN points to the line.)

ELEANOR: Thank you. *(After she signs.)* Don't forget to…

JONATHAN: …mark it in the ledger?

ELEANOR: That's right. And put today's date…
(Handing it to him) Here you go.

JONATHAN: Thank you.

ELEANOR: You're very welcome.

(JONATHAN *takes the checkbook back to the table, looks at the check again, hesitates, but ultimately rips it in half and throws it away.*)

ELEANOR: Boy, am I hungry.

JONATHAN: (*Starting for the door; mixed up himself.*) Why don't I go see what's holding up Rosalia.

ELEANOR: We shouldn't put too much pressure on the new girl. She's still getting used to things.

JONATHAN: Right. (*He sits in his chair, exhausted.*)

ELEANOR: Gorgeous flowers.

JONATHAN: And they smell nice too.

(*Beat*)

ELEANOR: What about a nice paisley tie?

(*Black out*)

Scene 7

(*A coffee shop.* JONATHAN *sits and waits. After some moments,* GREGORY *enters with his briefcase, looking much more businesslike than he did before. There's also something more rigid in his posture.*)

GREGORY: Sorry I couldn't take you to lunch this time—it's been a crazy day at the office. I only have a few minutes.

JONATHAN: Anything exciting?

GREGORY: Just your average spoiled American family squabbling over inheritance; only in this case, the father's not even dead. Second marriage: two sets of kids. The first batch always gets screwed.

JONATHAN: How's that?

GREGORY: The second wife's usually the same age as the first kids. All the money is put in trust for her to live off—by the time she's dead, so are the first children.

JONATHAN: What about the first wife?

GREGORY: She doesn't figure into the equation. Anyway, I have no time to beat around the bush.

JONATHAN: Is something wrong?

GREGORY: Do you know why it's a bush?

JONATHAN: No.

GREGORY: I'm reading this book about the history of English idioms, and some of them go back hundreds of years. It's amazing.

JONATHAN: There must be many wonderful Russian expressions.

GREGORY: They all have to do with drinking or suicide. But that's beside the point—or is it besides the point?

JONATHAN: Beside.

GREGORY: *(Takes note in his little book)* I'm under a lot pressure from my firm to improve my English.

JONATHAN: So, what's so important?

GREGORY: First of all, I just want to say that, on a personal note, I think what you've been doing for Eleanor these past few weeks has been admirable.

JONATHAN: Now you have me worried.

GREGORY: Oh, no, it's nothing like that.

JONATHAN: Like what?

GREGORY: Like nothing. It's just that after the whole Victoria affair, the family is suddenly more concerned with her well-being.

JONATHAN: You mean their well-being.

GREGORY: Touché. So everything's okay with her?

JONATHAN: Who?

GREGORY: Eleanor.

JONATHAN: Oh, yeah. She's been a little more scattered than usual, but otherwise she seems fine.

GREGORY: And no problems with Rosalia?

JONATHAN: Actually, I think Eleanor's starting to take to her. The other day her little boy came over to play-

GREGORY: Whose?

JONATHAN: Rosalia's.

GREGORY: Rosalia's son was over at Eleanor's?

JONATHAN: It was after school and she had nobody to look after him.

GREGORY: That's not a good idea.

JONATHAN: But you should've seen Eleanor; she was a different person.

GREGORY: The family is extremely suspicious of any outsiders right now, so please, no mixing business with pleasure, all right?

JONATHAN: I don't see the harm.

GREGORY: Attachment. Private schools. Braces. College tuition. The family does not want to go down this road again.

JONATHAN: Perhaps it would be best if you told her.

GREGORY: Fine… And no more mentions of Victoria?

JONATHAN: Occasionally, she gets the names mixed up. But I think she's finally given up the prospect of her return.

GREGORY: Good. Anyway, the family's concern translates into us making sure nothing like this happens again.

JONATHAN: Understandable. I've already taken steps to make certain of that.

GREGORY: Such as…

JONATHAN: Charge accounts have been set up at the supermarket, drugstore and a fruit and vegetable stand. I've also put the paper, cable, heating/electric and phone on her credit card, which I pay off through the Internet at the end of the month. But if the family feels more comfortable monitoring the situation, I'm happy to pass on the codes.

GREGORY: That might be a good idea—just so we have a system of balances and checks.

JONATHAN: Of course.

GREGORY: And you've been spending more time with Eleanor?

JONATHAN: Obviously.

GREGORY: But there are no problems with Rosalia?

JONATHAN: No. It's more about making her feel comfortable in her new environment.

GREGORY: You mean with Rosalia?

JONATHAN: Yes. Rosalia's English isn't quite up to par, and I'm not so sure how good her reading skills are.

GREGORY: Why does she have to read?

JONATHAN: Victoria used to read the paper to Eleanor every morning. Sort of a ritual. She likes to know what's going on in the world.

GREGORY: So you do that now?

JONATHAN: I'm trying to keep things as normal as possible.

GREGORY: Good... Everyday?

JONATHAN: When I can. I try to pass by as often as I can—it's on my way to the Conservatory.

GREGORY: So, you've been putting in more days.

JONATHAN: More days, shorter hours.

GREGORY: Any reason?

JONATHAN: I just told you.

GREGORY: Right...

JONATHAN: You said you didn't want to beat around the bush.

GREGORY: You're right. Katherine is coming to town next week, and, well, since the whole episode with Victoria, she wants to see the books.

JONATHAN: No problem.

GREGORY: I've taken the liberty of looking at the recent statements from the bank, the cashed checks—I hope you don't mind?

JONATHAN: Not at all.

GREGORY: I wanted to make sure there were no surprises, if you know what I mean.

JONATHAN: Of course. Thank you for doing that.

GREGORY: You're welcome. But I have to say...there were a few surprises. *(Pause)* Do you have anything to say?

JONATHAN: I'm not quite sure what you're getting at.

GREGORY: It's just that the amount of checks being paid out to you has increased.

JONATHAN: As just mentioned, I've been spending more time with Eleanor, so there are more hours.

GREGORY: Understandable.

JONATHAN: And, I suppose, I've also taken it upon myself to play a greater role in everyday matters as we transition into the new *strategem*.

GREGORY: Groceries?

JONATHAN: Sometimes.

GREGORY: But not always at the supermarket where the charge account's set up.

JONATHAN: Actually there have been a few times when I had to—

GREGORY: Four.

JONATHAN: What?

GREGORY: Four times you wrote checks to yourself and scribbled "groceries" in the memo box.

JONATHAN: *(A little off guard)* Yes, that's about right— when I was coming from school, and I was short on time, I picked up a few things near the Conservatory.

GREGORY: $38.23, $41.06, $48.56 and $64.45.

JONATHAN: You have amounts?

GREGORY: As I said, I have to answer to the family.

JONATHAN: You've made that clear a few times already.

GREGORY: I need to make sure there are no surprises. Do you remember what you bought for $64.45 on Friday, April 29th?

JONATHAN: Well, if my recollection is correct, that day I picked up a bottle of red wine to have with our dinner.

GREGORY: *(Surprised)* You had dinner with Eleanor?

JONATHAN: Yes, on several occasions. Especially during the transition. She was quite distraught and wasn't eating Angelica's food.

GREGORY: What were the rest of the groceries?

JONATHAN: That was it. Oh—and a grilled cheese sandwich for a homeless man. But I deducted that from my future wages. It's all marked down in the book.

GREGORY: So you spent $60 dollars on a bottle of wine for Eleanor?

JONATHAN: I thought it would be a treat for her. A couple of days earlier we had read an article in the paper about wine country in the Sonoma Valley.

GREGORY: You have to be careful with things like this.

JONATHAN: She really enjoyed it.

GREGORY: Maybe, but looking at it from the outside…it crosses a line.

JONATHAN: I suppose, if I were to be the suspicious type, I can see your point. I won't do it again.

GREGORY: Good. Now, on the same day, there's a check written out to you for $183.47.

JONATHAN: Yes.

GREGORY: What's that for?

JONATHAN: Her old radio broke—I went to buy a new one.

GREGORY: But the check was written out to you?

JONATHAN: I didn't have enough time to go back and forth, so I picked it up on my way home and brought it the next morning.

GREGORY: But you had enough time to share a bottle of wine?

JONATHAN: The radio broke in the evening. You can check the time on the receipt.

GREGORY: And you have that?

JONATHAN: Of course.

GREGORY: I'll need it.

JONATHAN: ...Are you accusing me of something, because if you are, I'd appreciate it if you just came out and said it.

GREGORY: I'm telling you that Katherine can make things very difficult for me, and the last thing I need right now is for her to go over my head and jeopardize my chances of making partner. Understand?

JONATHAN: Yes.

GREGORY: I can't afford any problems. I've sacrificed too much for this.

JONATHAN: Understood.

GREGORY: So, in the future, it's better for you to get Eleanor to write out the check to the store and then fill in the numbers later.

JONATHAN: It's just I didn't know which store I was going to buy the radio fro—

GREGORY: Please don't argue with me.

JONATHAN: Fine.

(GREGORY *looks through his notes.*)

GREGORY: (*Suddenly lightening up; almost out of duty.*) By the way, do you want a coffee?

JONATHAN: No.

GREGORY: Blueberry Danish? My treat. It's got real blueberries.

(JONATHAN *just stares at* GREGORY.)

GREGORY: Right. Well, I also noticed that some of the checks had amounts that were different from the usual multiples of fifteen—which is what you get per hour.

JONATHAN: True. Part of that is subway fare.

GREGORY: To get to Eleanor's?

JONATHAN: To and from, yes. She felt that since I was coming more often I should be compensated for my transportation.

GREGORY: *(Challenging him)* Did she…

JONATHAN: Yes.

GREGORY: You really should've cleared that with me.

JONATHAN: Sorry, it didn't seem like very much.

GREGORY: If it wasn't very much, why did you tack it on?

JONATHAN: Fine, I'll pay it back.

GREGORY: That's okay, but the next time you—

JONATHAN: I don't want any suspicions hovering over—

GREGORY: Forget about it! …I mean at least you didn't hire a car service.

JONATHAN: Actually, there was one instance—late at night—when I took a cab home.

GREGORY: *(Almost as if he knew already)* What were you doing at Eleanor's late at night?

JONATHAN: She wanted to watch the fights.

GREGORY: What fights?

JONATHAN: Boxing. There was a heavyweight fight on T V. I thought it would be fun for us to watch it together. I also had a few friends from the Conservatory come over.

GREGORY: You had friends come over to Eleanor's apartment?

JONATHAN: From the Conservatory. She really enjoyed herself.

GREGORY: Did you charge her for your time?

JONATHAN: Of course not.

GREGORY: And the fight?

JONATHAN: What about it?

GREGORY: Wasn't it pay-per-view?

JONATHAN: You have to order it, yes.

GREGORY: Did you and your friends make Eleanor pay for your boxing, yes or no?

JONATHAN: I assume it was charged to her account.

GREGORY: So she called in the order herself?

JONATHAN: I did.

GREGORY: And that cost?

JONATHAN: Fifty-five dollars.

(GREGORY *scribbles something in his book.*)

GREGORY: More than sixty with tax.

JONATHAN: Tax was included.

GREGORY: Now, that's a bargain!

JONATHAN: Look, I was hired to come in once a week and write a few checks.

GREGORY: Exactly my point.

JONATHAN: But then you dropped this on me.

GREGORY: No, you took it upon yourself.

JONATHAN: What do you want me to do? Not care?

GREGORY: Is that what you call it?

JONATHAN: You turn an old woman's world upside-down and expect everything to proceed as normal? It's not all about numbers. She's a person, with feelings, and she needs me right now!

GREGORY: What could she possibly have needed you for…six hours…on …. (*Looking at his notes*) May 16th.

JONATHAN: May 16th?

GREGORY: A Tuesday. I believe it rained like a bucket.

JONATHAN: Oh. I had to take her to the gynecologist.

GREGORY: Couldn't Rosalia do that? Seems like more of a womanly thing to do.

JONATHAN: I suppose, if we wanted to risk Eleanor slipping while getting in and out of the cab and cracking her head open, we could've gotten by.

GREGORY: And that took six hours?

JONATHAN: Actually, it took seven.

GREGORY: Why didn't you charge accordingly? Were you offering some kind of discount?

JONATHAN: *(Getting up to leave)* Okay, I think I'm done here...

GREGORY: June 1st.

(JONATHAN stops in his tracks.)

GREGORY: Nineteen hundred dollars...On top of the two and a half hours. Check number 302...

JONATHAN: *(With a forced impression of disbelief)* She wanted to buy me a suit.

GREGORY: A thousand dollar suit. Who are you, Yo-Yo Ma?

JONATHAN: It was also for a white shirt, shoes...a tie... It was for my birthday.

GREGORY: Isn't your birthday *(Peeking at his notes)* ...in October?

JONATHAN: Paul Stein got a suit.

GREGORY: Ah, well, if Paul Stein got a suit...

JONATHAN: It gave Eleanor pleasure to buy me a suit. She wanted to express her appreciation by buying me a gift. Is something wrong with that?! *(He is suddenly aware of how similar his words sound to VICTORIA's.)*

GREGORY: You tell me.

JONATHAN: It's not the way you're making it seem.

GREGORY: I think it would be best if you stayed away from Eleanor's from now on.

JONATHAN: Don't do this to her.

GREGORY: I'll be notifying the building's management.

JONATHAN: Gregory, listen—

GREGORY: The doormen will also be informed.

JONATHAN: Please.

GREGORY: Maybe send her a postcard: something to the effect of forgetting to renew your student visa and getting deported back to Canada.

JONATHAN: *(Backtracking)* Okay, look, I admit, the suit was a mistake. I'll pay it back. I didn't want to take it…

(GREGORY just nods his head.)

JONATHAN: Fine… You're right…I made a mistake. I was weak, and there should be severe consequences for my actions. There is absolutely no excuse for what I did… But please, for Eleanor's sake, at least let me visit her. We've become very close. I don't have any grandparents who are still alive.

GREGORY: I'm just curious, when your father used to bring flowers to his mother for the holidays, or her birthday, or maybe for no special reason at all except to make her smile…do you think he ever charged her for them?

JONATHAN: Okay, look—

GREGORY: *(Reading from his book)* Venus Fly-Trap Florists: Forty-six dollars, fifty-six cents…

JONATHAN: That was the only time.

GREGORY: Fluorescence: —nice play on words—ninety-seven dollars, ten cents...

JONATHAN: It was Mother's Day and I was broke—

GREGORY: A wonderful gift.

JONATHAN: She deserved to have someone look after her.

GREGORY: Oh, you certainly did that.

JONATHAN: You can't stop me from seeing her!

GREGORY: I can do whatever I want. *(Standing up; with pride)* I'm her accountant! *(He is about to walk out, but has one last thing to say.)* Incidentally, when I got back to the office after the first time we met, I mentioned to my colleague that you had ordered the cheapest thing on the menu. I was actually quite encouraged by this as it gave me the impression that you had respect for other people's money. But this colleague of mine, he expressed concern. He said that he would feel a lot better if you had ordered the second cheapest thing on the menu—that way it would show that you still had respect for other people's money, but it wasn't the only thing you thought about.

JONATHAN: And our little three hundred dollar lobster lunch...who exactly paid for that?

(GREGORY feels exposed himself, and abruptly exits.)

(JONATHAN puts his head between his knees.)

(Black out)

Scene 8

(ELEANOR *sits alone, trying to read a newspaper with her magnifying glass.* KATHERINE, *her daughter, approaches from behind. She's somewhat disheveled, poorly dressed, and seems fragile or unsure of herself. She decides that maybe it be best if she leaves, but a moment later she's back.)*

KATHERINE: Hello, Eleanor.

ELEANOR: Who's that?

KATHERINE: It's Katy.

ELEANOR: Katherine? What are you doing here?

KATHERINE: I've come to visit you.

ELEANOR: Did I know you were coming?

KATHERINE: We spoke last week.

ELEANOR: *(Not really remembering)* That's right… Are you staying awhile?

KATHERINE: Just a few days.

ELEANOR: Should I ask the girl to make up your bed?

KATHERINE: I've booked a room at the Beacon. Thought it would be easier.

ELEANOR: Suit yourself.

KATHERINE: But she seems very nice.

ELEANOR: Who?

KATHERINE: The new girl.

(No answer)

KATHERINE: Raoul, from downstairs says hello.

ELEANOR: How is good old Raoul?

KATHERINE: He hasn't changed a bit. A little grayer, but who isn't.

ELEANOR: Some people are like that.

KATHERINE: I'll never forget when he first started working here, I was sixteen, and before he opened the door for me to get into a cab, he would stick his head into the passenger window and warn the driver to, "take good care of my *yaughter*." As the cab pulled away, I'd see him pretending to scribble down the license plate number of the taxi.

ELEANOR: Wasn't that nice of him.

KATHERINE: Yes it was. His son, Eddie, just got an athletic scholarship to Princeton.

ELEANOR: Good for him.

KATHERINE: Apparently, he's also very intelligent. Straight As. Raoul gets tears in his eyes just talking about him.

ELEANOR: That's wonderful. Maybe I should send him a little something.

KATHERINE: *(A little aggressive)* Didn't you just give him a bonus for Christmas?

(ELEANOR picks up her magnifying glass and continues reading.)

KATHERINE: I hope I'm not interrupting anything important.

ELEANOR: No, no, just catching up on the news. Are you staying for long?

KATHERINE: Just a few days.

ELEANOR: I'll have the girl make up the bed.

KATHERINE: I'm not sure if I can get out of my reservation.

ELEANOR: For what?

KATHERINE: The Beacon Hotel.

ELEANOR: Suit yourself.

(Pause)

KATHERINE: Karl and the children say hello. They wanted to come, but it's right in the middle of the semester.

ELEANOR: How are they doing?

KATHERINE: Very well. Karl just started teaching at a new high school—right outside of Dachau of all places; Nicholas has finally put the divorce behind him and is finishing up a special course to sell pet insurance, and Sabine has gone to live in Berlin and wants to make music videos.

ELEANOR: Isn't that nice.

KATHERINE: I guess she takes after Uncle Joe.

ELEANOR: What's it like outside?

KATHERINE: Very pleasant. Would you like to go for a walk?

ELEANOR: Don't get out much these days.

KATHERINE: That's too bad.

ELEANOR: Not really. *(She continues trying to read the newspaper with her magnifying glass.)*

KATHERINE: I got you these flowers…

(ELEANOR gives them the once over but doesn't think much of them.)

ELEANOR: Thank you.

KATHERINE: Should I put them in a vase?

ELEANOR: Nah, you can leave them on top of the table. The girl will take care of them.

(KATHERINE leaves the flowers.)

KATHERINE: They have a nice smell to them too.

(ELEANOR grabs a Kleenex and blows her nose.)

KATHERINE: I was sorry to hear about Victoria…

ELEANOR: *(Suddenly alert)* What did you hear from Victoria?

KATHERINE: I was just saying that I was sorry to hear what happened. *(No reaction)* I guess you never really know.

ELEANOR: About what?

KATHERINE: About people.

ELEANOR: I'm not following you.

KATHERINE: Never mind. I think I'm a little jet-lagged.

ELEANOR: You look tired. When did you fly in?

KATHERINE: Just a few hours ago. Those seats in economy are so small, it's almost enough to make you want to take a boat.

ELEANOR: Did I know you were coming?

KATHERINE: *(A little confrontational)* Yes, you knew I was coming.

ELEANOR: Must've slipped my mind.

KATHERINE: *(Quietly; to herself)* I'm so tired of this.

ELEANOR: *(Picking it up)* Yes, you look tired.

KATHERINE: I heard you the first time.

ELEANOR: Oh?

(Uncomfortable silence)

KATHERINE: *(More to see her mother's reaction)* Well, I guess I should probably go out and pick something up for dinner.

ELEANOR: Didn't they feed you on the plane?

KATHERINE: The food was inedible.

ELEANOR: Too bad.

(KATHERINE *just stares at* ELEANOR *as if she's trying to read her.* ELEANOR *strains to read a name on the pad, which she scribbled down earlier.*)

ELEANOR: Who's Ralph?

KATHERINE: Ralph? …Ralph Samuelson? He was Adam's friend. The little boy who drowned at the lake.

ELEANOR: That's the one.

KATHERINE: Whatever made you think of him?

ELEANOR: He was a bright kid…used to sit at the piano and play anything you whistled to him.

KATHERINE: He had perfect pitch.

ELEANOR: What a shame.

KATHERINE: It was the first time I saw you cry.

ELEANOR: It was a sad day. Your father cried.

KATHERINE: Oh, he always cried: sad movies, concerts, my wedding. But you…I remember that summer, a part of me wished it had been me that drowned just so you would cry for me.

ELEANOR: *(With a chuckle)* Isn't that something…

(It's not the response KATHERINE *is looking for.)*

KATHERINE: But you didn't like me.

ELEANOR: *(Unconvincingly)* I liked you *(enough)*.

KATHERINE: *(Despite* ELEANOR*)* Daddy liked me.

ELEANOR: Yes he did. You were always his little Princess.

KATHERINE: But he liked Adam too.

ELEANOR: Sure… *(Possessive)* But Adam was mine.

KATHERINE: Why was it like that?

*(*ELEANOR *picks up her magnifying glass and starts reading again.)*

ELEANOR: ...What day is it today?

KATHERINE: Thursday.

ELEANOR: I think I'm supposed to call somebody.

KATHERINE: Who?

ELEANOR: If I knew I'd be calling him, wouldn't I.

(Beat)

KATHERINE: I spoke with Gregory on my way here.

ELEANOR: Who?

KATHERINE: The accountant.

ELEANOR: How is good old Gregory?

KATHERINE: He seemed a little down.

ELEANOR: Oh?

KATHERINE: Apparently, they passed him over for partner again.

ELEANOR: That's too bad. Maybe he should move to another office.

KATHERINE: He's not really that type of person.

ELEANOR: What type of person?

KATHERINE: Someone who takes risks...

ELEANOR: I'm sure he'll bounce back.

KATHERINE: He feels it's best if you're not burdened with having to write any more checks.

ELEANOR: Oh?

KATHERINE: He says there's a way you can have all your financial needs taken care of.

ELEANOR: I take care of my needs.

KATHERINE: Of course you do. But this is more for day-to-day needs. It can all be done by auto-pay.

ELEANOR: Auto?

KATHERINE: Automatic payment. Basically, the bank pays all your bills and salaries without you having to do anything.

ELEANOR: *(Feigning excitement)* Isn't that something.

KATHERINE: I've been meaning to do it for myself in Munich. It also saves money on postage.

ELEANOR: Well, that's good. The mail is getting so expensive. Cost me six cents to send a postcard to my sister-in-law in California.

KATHERINE: There's obviously some paperwork that needs to be signed, giving permission to the bank to process the transactions.

ELEANOR: Which bank?

KATHERINE: Your bank.

ELEANOR: What about my bank?

KATHERINE: They will pay all your bills.

ELEANOR: Well, tell them to mail me the information, and I'll look it over.

KATHERINE: Actually... *(Sneakily producing another form from her pocket)* I happen to have the form with me.

ELEANOR: *(Suspicious)* What is that?

KATHERINE: The form to sign.

ELEANOR: What form?

KATHERINE: From the bank. Automatic payment. So, you'll have no worries.

ELEANOR: Oh?

KATHERINE: It will take a huge burden off your shoulders. Do you want to sign it?

ELEANOR: If that's what you need.

(KATHERINE *brings the form over and places it in front of* ELEANOR.)

KATHERINE: It's for your benefit, not mine.

(ELEANOR *takes her magnifying glass and tries to read it.*)

ELEANOR: That's a lot of words. What does it say?

KATHERINE: Just a lot of legal jargon.

ELEANOR: Oh?

KATHERINE: To protect them.

ELEANOR: Who?

KATHERINE: The bank.

ELEANOR: From what?

KATHERINE: Here, let me read it for you… (*She grabs the form and skims through it very quickly. Reading*) Ya-da-da-da…Okay. (*To* ELEANOR) Basically, it says you give them the right to act on your behalf.

ELEANOR: Who?

KATHERINE: (*Loosing her patience*) The bank!

ELEANOR: Right. (*Trying to read through her magnifying glass.*) Let me have a look.

KATHERINE: You just did.

ELEANOR: What does it say?

KATHERINE: I already told you!

(KATHERINE *puts the form in front of* ELEANOR *again.*)

ELEANOR: (*Suspicious*) I don't think I want to sign it anymore.

KATHERINE: Look, Mother, I can't be here all the time to make sure people aren't taking advantage of you.

ELEANOR: Nobody takes advantage of me.

KATHERINE: Fine. (*Taking the form back*) I thought it would make life easier for you, but if you don't want to sign, don't sign. You're not doing me any favors.

ELEANOR: I won't.

KATHERINE: I'm not going to worry anymore.

ELEANOR: Don't.

(KATHERINE *stares at* ELEANOR *in disbelief, then, forcefully, lays the form in front of her again.*)

KATHERINE: You're going to sign this paper, Mother, because I am sick and tired of you playing around with your money. You have three grandchildren—not to mention Karl and I—who get by on a skimpy teaching salary, and you hold your money over us like it's all some kind of game to you. Well, I've had enough of living with your indifference. You are going to sign this form!

(ELEANOR *sees no way out and is about to sign but hesitates again.*)

ELEANOR: What am I signing?

(KATHERINE *shoots* ELEANOR *a threatening look.*)

(ELEANOR *signs the paper. When she finishes, she looks up and sees that* KATHERINE *has produced another form from her pocket. This one has several pages and is on legal paper.*)

KATHERINE: And one more...

(KATHERINE *places the forms in front of* ELEANOR.)

ELEANOR: What's this?

KATHERINE: They need two copies.

ELEANOR: *(Holding it up; trying to see)* This one looks different from the other one.

KATHERINE: It says the same thing.

ELEANOR: There are more pages.

KATHERINE: I am not going to go through this again.

ELEANOR: I'm not signing it.

KATHERINE: Fine. Don't!

ELEANOR: I won't...

(KATHERINE *lunges forward, forcefully grabbing*
ELEANOR's *hand and making her scribble her signature on
the bottom of the form.* ELEANOR *gives a struggle, but she is
no match for* KATHERINE.)

(KATHERINE *has* ELEANOR's *signature on the form, but she
is somewhat shocked at her own actions.*)

(ELEANOR *just sits in her chair and looks straight ahead.*)

(*After some moments…*)

KATHERINE: (*Struggling with her emotions.*) I don't know
why you made me do that… It's not fair of you to
make me do that…

ELEANOR: …

KATHERINE: Are you still my mommy?

ELEANOR: …

KATHERINE: Mom?

(ELEANOR *looks up at* KATHERINE *ever slightly and gives
her daughter a look of such hatred that it's even startling to
herself.*)

(KATHERINE—*in an effort not to lose it altogether—smooths
out her clothes and collects herself.*)

KATHERINE: Well…I'll just…ah… Why don't I… Maybe
I can pick something up for dinner… Would you like
that?

ELEANOR: …

KATHERINE: Do they still have those bad movies
on Channel 11? We can pull out the trays and…
sandwiches while we— …Would you like that?…I'll
go get the sandwiches and we can—…

ELEANOR: (*Forcing herself to make a concession*) Sure.

(*A big smile comes over* KATHERINE's *face. She starts to
leave but then goes back to kiss* ELEANOR *on the head from
behind.*)

ELEANOR: Who's that?

KATHERINE: It's still your little Katy.

ELEANOR: Katherine? What are you doing here?

KATHERINE: You know exactly what I'm doing here.
I've come to spend time with you.

ELEANOR: Isn't that nice.

KATHERINE: Yes it is…

(KATHERINE *waits for more, but nothing comes. Her smile
extinguishes and she exits.*)

(ELEANOR *goes back to trying to read with the magnifying
glass, but suddenly drops it on the floor. She tries to retrieve
it, but comes up empty-handed, and somehow manages to get
out of her chair, down on her knees, and tries to look for it.*)

ELEANOR: Darn it…Victoria! …Is there anyone out
there?… *(Muttering to herself.)* …What's her name
again?… *(Continues searching)* …Lolita? No…Rose? …
Rose bushes? …Lilly-Rose ?…Oh, hell… *(Continues
searching)*

(Fade to black)

END OF PLAY